INSIDE THE NBA

MILWAUKEE BUCKS

BY WILL GRAVES

SportsZone
An Imprint of Abdo Publishing
abdobooks.com

abdobooks.com

Published by Abdo Publishing, a division of ABDO, PO Box 398166, Minneapolis, Minnesota 55439. Copyright © 2023 by Abdo Consulting Group, Inc. International copyrights reserved in all countries. No part of this book may be reproduced in any form without written permission from the publisher. SportsZone™ is a trademark and logo of Abdo Publishing.

Printed in the United States of America, North Mankato, Minnesota.
052022
092022

Cover Photo: Kathy Willens/AP Images
Interior Photos: Melinda Nagy/Shutterstock Images, 1; Jonathan Daniel/Getty Images Sport/Getty Images, 4, 13, 41; Andrew D. Bernstein/NBAE/Getty Images, 7; Justin Casterline/Getty Images Sport/Getty Images, 9; Christian Peterson/Getty Images Sport/Getty Images, 10; Focus on Sport/Getty Images, 14, 24, 26, 34; Focus on Sport/Getty Images Sport/Getty Images, 17, 19, 37; Jonathan Daniel/Allsport/Getty Images Sport/Getty Images, 20; Sporting News/Getty Images, 21; Elsa/Getty Images Sport/Getty Images, 23; Todd Warshaw/Icon Sportswire/Getty Images, 29; Layne Murdoch/NBAE/Getty Images, 30; Jacob Kupferman/AP Images, 33; Jeff Haynes/AFP/Getty Images, 39

Editor: Charlie Beattie
Series Designer: Joshua Olson

Library of Congress Control Number: 2021951660

Publisher's Cataloging-in-Publication Data

Names: Graves, Will, author.
Title: Milwaukee Bucks / by Will Graves
Description: Minneapolis, Minnesota: Abdo Publishing, 2023 | Series: Inside the NBA | Includes online resources and index.
Identifiers: ISBN 9781532198342 (lib. bdg.) | ISBN 9781098271992 (ebook)
Subjects: LCSH: Milwaukee Bucks (Basketball team)--Juvenile literature. | Basketball--Juvenile literature. | Professional sports--Juvenile literature. | Sports franchises--Juvenile literature.
Classification: DDC 796.32364--dc23

TABLE OF CONTENTS

CHAPTER ONE
REACHING NEW HEIGHTS 4

CHAPTER TWO
BUCKING FOR TITLES 14

CHAPTER THREE
BEST OF THE BUCKS 24

CHAPTER FOUR
MILWAUKEE MOMENTS 34

TIMELINE 42
TEAM FACTS 44
TEAM TRIVIA 45
GLOSSARY 46
MORE INFORMATION 47
ONLINE RESOURCES 47
INDEX 48
ABOUT THE AUTHOR 48

CHAPTER ONE

REACHING NEW HEIGHTS

The Milwaukee Bucks were in trouble. They were locked in a tight battle with the Phoenix Suns late in Game 5 of the 2021 National Basketball Association (NBA) Finals. The best-of-seven series was tied 2–2. With just over three minutes to go, the Bucks had been cruising behind a double-digit lead. But now, with less than 30 seconds left, Milwaukee was clinging to a 120–119 edge. Even worse, the Suns had the ball.

The crowd at Phoenix Suns Arena was exploding as Suns guard Devin Booker walked the ball across half-court. One basket would complete a miraculous comeback for Phoenix—and a terrible collapse for Milwaukee. As the teams set up for this all-important possession, more than just a 3–2 series lead was on the line. Three days later, the Bucks and Suns would head back to Milwaukee for Game 6. If the Bucks held here, they would head home one win away from a championship.

Giannis Antetokounmpo was the Bucks' leading scorer throughout the 2021 playoffs.

If they didn't, they would wonder how this game had gotten away.

A CINDERELLA PAIRING

At the start of the season, not many predicted the 2021 NBA Finals would feature Milwaukee and Phoenix. The Suns had finished just 34–39 a season before. Milwaukee was enjoying a fifth-straight winning record. But the Bucks had yet to advance past the conference finals. Neither team had reached the NBA Finals in decades. Phoenix's last appearance was in 1993. Milwaukee had not been back since 1974.

However, both teams had talented rosters. The Suns were led by Booker, one of the game's budding superstars. They also added veteran point guard Chris Paul before the season. He had been one of the best at his position for nearly 20 years. Paul's addition helped the team improve to 51–21 in 2020–21.

Meanwhile, Milwaukee also had one of the game's best stars.

"Middle" Man

Giannis Antetokounmpo wasn't the only member of the Bucks who endured a lot of losing early in his career. Khris Middleton and Antetokounmpo were teammates on the 2013–14 team that finished 15–67. Middleton made the Suns pay if they focused too much on Antetokounmpo. Armed with an accurate shot and the ability to score all over the floor, Middleton averaged 24 points a game during the Finals.

Antetokounmpo, *left,* **led the Bucks into the 2021 NBA Finals against star guard Devin Booker,** *right,* **and the Phoenix Suns.**

Forward Giannis Antetokounmpo arrived in Milwaukee in 2013 as a skinny, raw 18-year-old from Greece. By the time the 2021 NBA Finals began, Antetokounmpo was one of the best players on the planet. His chiseled 6-foot-11-inch, 242-pound frame and guard skills earned him the nickname "the Greek Freak." He was a fixture on the All-Star team. Antetokounmpo also earned the 2020 NBA Most Valuable Player (MVP) Award after leading the Bucks to the best record in the NBA. But his injury in the second round of the playoffs that year doomed the Bucks to a loss against the Miami Heat.

ON A MISSION

Antetokounmpo and his teammates vowed not to let history repeat itself in 2021. The Bucks got some payback by sweeping Miami in the first round of the playoffs. Milwaukee then rallied to beat the Brooklyn Nets in the semifinals, winning Game 7 on the road in overtime. It took six games for the Bucks to slide past the Atlanta Hawks in the Eastern Conference finals.

Beating the Suns would not be easy. The Suns cruised through the West playoffs. Phoenix also had home-court advantage. That showed in the first two games when the Suns put up a pair of double-digit victories.

Milwaukee rebounded at home in Games 3 and 4. That set up a showdown back in Arizona for Game 5. Milwaukee knew it had to find a way to win a game in Phoenix, or the Bucks' title dreams would be dashed.

That looked like the case early on. Phoenix built a 16-point first-quarter lead. But the Bucks rallied in the second quarter. Point guard Jrue Holiday's 14 points helped Milwaukee surge to a 64–61 edge at the half. That lead only grew throughout most of the second half. Milwaukee led by 10 entering the fourth quarter. And the Bucks still led 120–112 with 2:23 to play.

At that point, things started to collapse for Milwaukee. Booker hit a layup on the next possession. He followed up with a three-pointer the next time down the floor. Paul then

Antetokounmpo drives past two Phoenix defenders for a layup.

Antetokounmpo throws down a lob from Jrue Holiday (21) at the end of Game 5.

trimmed Milwaukee's lead to just one point with a baseline drive for a score. After Holiday missed a shot with 31 seconds left, Booker grabbed the rebound.

THE LOB

With just over 20 seconds left, Booker made his move. From the right wing, he beat his defender to the middle and drove the lane. Antetokounmpo cut off his path. Booker double-clutched his shot as the Bucks forward towered over him.

Booker needed another option. He had picked up his dribble. Now he brought the ball down low and away from Antetokounmpo. Holiday saw an opening. The Milwaukee guard dove down from the three-point line and snatched it away.

As Holiday took off up court, he had a choice. The smart play was to hold the ball and wait for the Suns to foul him. But he also saw Antetokounmpo sprinting toward the basket. Paul was the only defender back for Phoenix. As Holiday reached the offensive

Best "Bud"

The Bucks might have been making their first NBA Finals appearance in 47 years, but head coach Mike Budenholzer was a regular. Budenholzer helped the San Antonio Spurs win four titles over 17 seasons as an assistant coach under Gregg Popovich from 1996 to 2013. He then became the head coach of the Atlanta Hawks. He arrived in Milwaukee in 2018. Three years later, he had a fifth ring to go with the four he had earned with the Spurs.

three-point line, he took a chance. The guard lobbed the ball toward his teammate. Antetokounmpo rose over Paul, grabbed the ball, and slammed it home—a gorgeous alley-oop. Paul threw both his hands out to try to foul Milwaukee's star. He did, but the contact did nothing to stop the dunk.

The clock showed 13 seconds. Milwaukee led 122–119. The Phoenix crowd was stunned into silence. The comeback had been snuffed out by Holiday's gamble and Antetokounmpo's dunk. After the Bucks secured the 123–119 win, Holiday was asked about his decision.

"Giannis took off and he was calling for the ball," Holiday said. "At that point, I just threw it as high as I could and only where Giannis could go get it."

MILWAUKEE MOMENTUM

Three days later, the teams took the court again at Fiserv Forum in Milwaukee. They were greeted by more than 17,000 screaming fans hoping to see the Bucks' first NBA title in exactly 50 years. The Greek Freak made sure they witnessed a celebration.

Antetokounmpo led the way with 50 points. He scored 33 of them in the second half as the Bucks turned around a 47–42 halftime deficit. Milwaukee pulled away late to win 105–98. Antetokounmpo averaged 35.2 points and 13.2 rebounds in the series. After the game, he was named Finals MVP.

Antetokounmpo added an NBA Finals MVP Award to his two regular-season MVP trophies after knocking off Phoenix.

The performance capped a long journey for both Antetokounmpo and Milwaukee. The Bucks had won just 15 games during his rookie season in 2013–14. Seven years later, they had leaped to the top of the basketball world.

CHAPTER TWO

BUCKING FOR TITLES

While the Bucks were new to Milwaukee in 1968–69, the NBA was not. In the 1950s, the city had the Milwaukee Hawks for four seasons. But the team had trouble winning and drawing fans. In 1955 the team's owners moved the struggling franchise to St. Louis. The Hawks eventually landed in Atlanta the same year the Bucks were born.

In the late 1960s, the NBA was growing. Several expansion teams joined the league starting in 1966. That year the Chicago Bulls were added. The Seattle SuperSonics and San Diego Rockets opened play in 1967–68. And the following year brought not only the Bucks but also the Phoenix Suns.

To name Milwaukee's new team, thousands of fans made suggestions. The owners settled on "Bucks" to honor the large white-tailed deer population in Wisconsin. The Bucks gave one of the fans who suggested the name a car.

Guard Jon McGlocklin averaged 12.6 points over eight seasons with the Bucks after being selected in the 1968 NBA expansion draft.

The Bucks finished just 27–55 during the 1968–69 season. But luck was soon on their side. At the time, the top pick in the NBA Draft was decided on a coin flip between the worst team in each division. The Bucks were last in the East. Their expansion partners, the Suns, were last in the West.

FROM LUCK TO LEGEND

The Suns chose heads. The coin came up tails. Just like that, Milwaukee had one of the best prospects in NBA history. That year the top prize was 7-foot-2-inch center Kareem Abdul-Jabbar of the University of California, Los Angeles.

Abdul-Jabbar immediately transformed the Bucks into contenders. Milwaukee's win total jumped from 27 to 56. The Bucks made the playoffs for the first time. Abdul-Jabbar was named the league's Rookie of the Year while averaging 28.8 points per game. The Bucks reached the East Division finals but lost to the New York Knicks.

Looking for a boost to put them over the top, the Bucks traded for superstar forward

Embry Enters

The Bucks made history in 1972 when they made Wayne Embry the first Black general manager in major American professional sports. A general manager's job includes drafting players, making trades, and negotiating contracts. Embry retired after an 11-year career in 1969. He held the general manager position for six years and put together the team that made the 1974 NBA Finals.

Oscar Robertson in April 1970. It was just the boost the Bucks needed. Robertson had been one of the NBA's best players with the Cincinnati Royals since 1960. With his veteran leadership and Abdul-Jabbar's dominant inside play, the Bucks cruised through the regular season with 66 wins. At one point they won 20 straight games, a league record at the time.

Guard Bob Dandridge (10) was a three-time All-Star in his nine seasons with the Bucks.

The team didn't slow down at all in the playoffs. Milwaukee rolled over all three of its opponents, losing only two games total. The Bucks finished off the championship run with a four-game sweep over the Baltimore Bullets. In just its third season, Milwaukee was on top of the league. It was the fastest rise by any expansion team in major American professional sports.

Milwaukee looked like it was built to last. Robertson was 32, but the rest of the team's stars were young. High-scoring small forward Bob Dandridge was only 23. Slick-shooting guard Jon McGlocklin was only 27. And Abdul-Jabbar was only 24.

NO HAPPY RETURNS

The Bucks did return to the Finals again in 1974 but lost to the Boston Celtics in seven games. Game 7 proved to be the last game of the 35-year-old Robertson's career. That was not a surprise. But Abdul-Jabbar was also ready to leave Milwaukee. The star center had grown up in New York City and gone to college in Los Angeles. He was having trouble relating to his Midwestern surroundings and requested a trade after the 1974–75 season. The Bucks ended up sending him to the Los Angeles Lakers in June 1975.

Over the next 14 years, Abdul-Jabbar won five titles and set the NBA career scoring record. Milwaukee struggled without him as the team went through several changes.

The next franchise legend to go was the team's original head coach, Larry Costello. He was fired after starting 3–15 in 1976–77. The Bucks hired Don Nelson as Costello's replacement. Nelson had been a member of the Celtics team that beat Milwaukee in the 1974 Finals. The Bucks didn't know it at the time, but they had just started one of the most successful coaching careers in history. Nelson led the Bucks from 1976 through 1987, claiming 540 of his 1,335 career wins there.

The next step was finding a star player. That came through the draft in 1979. At 6 feet, 4 inches, guard Sidney Moncrief was hardly Abdul-Jabbar. But he played bigger than his size. Over the next 10 years, Moncrief served as the motor that drove

Sidney Moncrief averaged a career-high 22.5 points per game in 1982–83.

Milwaukee to playoff berth after playoff berth. His play led the Bucks to seven straight Central Division titles. They reached the Eastern Conference finals three times in four seasons between 1982–83 and 1985–86 but could not get past the powerful Philadelphia 76ers or the Celtics.

Glenn Robinson dunks against the Indiana Pacers during a game in 2000.

THE BIG THREE ARRIVES

Moncrief left Milwaukee after the 1988–89 season. The Bucks made two more playoff appearances without him under new coach Del Harris. But the team finished 31–51 in 1991–92. It was the first losing season in Milwaukee in 13 years. But while the late 1970s offered a quick turnaround, the 1990s only got worse for the Bucks. The team suffered losing records for seven consecutive seasons.

Throughout the late 1990s, the Bucks slowly started putting solid young players on the floor. Small forward Glenn "Big Dog" Robinson was drafted first overall in 1994. Two years later, the Bucks swung a draft-day trade to get promising guard Ray Allen. Before the 1998–99 season, the Bucks added another successful coach, George Karl.

That year the NBA season was shortened to 50 games due to a lockout. But the Bucks managed to finish with a winning record at 28–22. They were back in the playoffs. Point guard Sam Cassell arrived in a trade that year. He gave Milwaukee another advantage alongside Robinson and Allen.

Everything came together in the 2000–01 season. But it didn't look that way from the start. The Bucks fell to 3–9 in late November after blowing a fourth-quarter lead to the Washington Wizards.

Sam Cassell played for eight NBA teams but spent 313 of his 993 career NBA games in a Milwaukee uniform.

Just when it seemed like Milwaukee was on the brink of collapse, the Bucks instead caught fire. Allen knocked down a team-record 202 three-pointers. Milwaukee finished the year with a 49–21 burst. That was enough to claim the Bucks' first Central Division title in 15 years.

The hot streak continued into the playoffs. The Bucks knocked off the Orlando Magic and Charlotte Hornets to reach the Eastern Conference finals before falling to Philadelphia in seven tough games.

MODERN MILWAUKEE

Once again, the Bucks could not sustain their momentum. They traded away Robinson after the following season. Karl, Allen, and Cassell all left in the next few years. A long stretch of forgettable seasons followed. The Bucks did not win another playoff round until 2019. Milwaukee was in that rut when it took a chance on a skinny, long-limbed teenager from Greece in the first round of the 2013 draft.

As Giannis Antetokounmpo grew comfortable in the NBA, Milwaukee's fortunes slowly changed. In 2015 the Bucks returned to the playoffs. In 2017 Antetokounmpo became an All-Star for the first time. In 2019 he won the first of back-to-back MVP awards.

By 2021 Antetokounmpo was the best player on the best team in basketball. The Bucks shook off five decades of frustration with a dazzling run to the Finals. Their triumph

Kohl Cashes In

The Bucks were in a bit of trouble in the 1980s when it looked like the franchise might leave town. Future US senator Herb Kohl swooped in to save the day. Kohl bought the Bucks for $18 million and promised to keep them in Milwaukee. His investment paid off. Kohl sold the team in 2014 for $550 million.

Giannis Antetokounmpo, *left*, **and Khris Middleton,** *right*, **huddle with Bucks head coach Mike Budenholzer.**

over Phoenix set off a celebration 50 years in the making and cemented Antetokounmpo's status as one of the franchise's all-time greats. Better yet, the then-26-year-old star had signed a contract in 2020 that would keep him in Milwaukee through the 2025–26 season. Not only were the Bucks on top, but they also looked like they might be able to finally stay there.

CHAPTER THREE

BEST OF THE BUCKS

There had been other great centers in the NBA before Kareem Abdul-Jabbar arrived. Most of them excelled on either offense or defense, but not both. Abdul-Jabbar dominated at each end of the floor. He was a nearly unstoppable scorer. Abdul-Jabbar's signature shot was his "skyhook." With his long arms, Abdul-Jabbar's hook shot was launched so far above his head that opposing players could not block it. One opponent said the shot looked like it was coming down from outer space. He was also a capable passer and could gobble up rebounds and swat away opponents' shots with ease.

Abdul-Jabbar stayed in Milwaukee for only six seasons before he was traded to the Los Angeles Lakers. Most NBA fans remember him best as center for the Lakers dynasty teams of the 1980s. But he spent enough time in Milwaukee to create

Kareem Abdul-Jabbar's length and athletic ability made him a devastating force in the NBA.

Oscar Robertson, *right*, looks to drive during a game against the Los Angeles Lakers.

a winning legacy. The city spent the next 50 years looking for another star that bright.

A decade before Abdul-Jabbar took the NBA by storm, Oscar Robertson did the same. He entered the league in 1960–61 with the Cincinnati Royals. In addition to scoring, he was also one of the game's best passers and rebounders. He averaged double figures in points, rebounds, and assists in 1961–62. No player had done that before. By the time he came to Milwaukee in 1970–71, Robertson wasn't putting up those kinds of numbers. But he was still one of the NBA's best guards. He still averaged 19.4 points and 8.2 assists during Milwaukee's title season.

Most importantly, Robertson won games. In the four years he played for Milwaukee, the team was a combined 248–80. The year after he retired, the Bucks finished 38–44, even though they still had Abdul-Jabbar.

SID THE SQUID

Most players who are great scorers don't worry too much about playing defense. Sidney Moncrief was not most players. The 6-foot-4-inch guard could fill up the basket, but where he really excelled was locking down opponents. Moncrief was a five-time All-Star for the Bucks in the 1980s. The NBA introduced the Defensive Player of the Year Award in 1983. "Sid the Squid" won the first two ever handed out.

Moncrief didn't take the Bucks to the playoffs every year

Dandy Don

Don Nelson was just 36 years old when the Bucks hired him as head coach in 1976. He guided Milwaukee to seven 50-win seasons during his 10 full seasons on the bench. He was named NBA Coach of the Year twice. After winning 540 games for the Bucks, he had two stints with the Golden State Warriors and one each with the New York Knicks and Dallas Mavericks. Though he never won an NBA title, Nelson retired as the winningest coach in NBA history in 2010.

during the 1980s by himself. Small forward Marques Johnson averaged 21 points per game over seven seasons in Milwaukee. He made four All-Star teams.

The Bucks made the tough decision in 1984 to trade Johnson, Junior Bridgeman, and Harvey Catchings to the Los Angeles Clippers. The Bucks received young forward Terry Cummings and guards Ricky Pierce and Craig Hodges. The deal worked out. Cummings made the All-Star team twice during the 1980s. He left the team in a 1989 trade with the San Antonio Spurs. But the veteran returned for one year toward the end of his career and spent the 1995–96 season back in Milwaukee.

THE BIG THREE AND BEYOND

Glenn Robinson was given the nickname "Big Dog" by the arena janitor during his college days at Purdue University. It fit for a player who stood 6 feet, 7 inches and weighed a muscular 225 pounds. But Robinson was more than just a bruiser. The two-time All-Star was also a solid shooter from anywhere on the floor. The Bucks made him the top pick of the 1994 draft. It took several seasons and some help, but Robinson started Milwaukee's turnaround in the late 1990s.

Much of that help came from one of the NBA's best-ever shooters. Guard Ray Allen joined Robinson in Milwaukee before his rookie season in 1996. The three-point shot is a key weapon

Ray Allen averaged over 20 points per game in each of his final three and a half seasons with the Bucks.

for NBA teams now. The 6-foot-5-inch Allen was one of the first players to bomb away from outside the arc. He made 202 three-pointers in 2000–01 as the Bucks reached the Eastern Conference finals. A year later, he led the league with 229.

Feeding Robinson and Allen was veteran point guard Sam Cassell. The Bucks were Cassell's fifth team since joining the NBA in 1993. He averaged career-high 9.0 assists along with

Michael Redd left the Bucks in 2011 as the team's fourth all-time leading scorer.

18.2 points per game in 1999–00. The next year he nearly duplicated those numbers as the "Big Three" carried Milwaukee within a game of the NBA Finals. By the time Cassell left the team in 2003, he was considered one of the league's best point guards.

Michael Redd was on the team when the Bucks made their run in 2000–01, but just barely. The left-handed guard had been a second-round pick the summer before. He played only six games all season and scored 13 total points. It certainly didn't look like Milwaukee had a future star on its hands. But Redd continued to grow. By the 2003–04 season, the Big Three was gone, and Redd was ready. He started every game that year and averaged 21.7 points per game. The 6-foot-6 Redd led Milwaukee to a surprise playoff berth and made the All-Star team in the process.

His career didn't peak there. In 2006–07 Redd averaged a career-high 26.7 points per game. Only four players averaged more that season.

FEAR THESE DEER

Giannis Antetokounmpo's road to the NBA began with an email in 2013. A scout from the New Orleans Hornets saw tape of the raw teenager going end-to-end for a dunk while playing in his native country, Greece. Antetokounmpo's numbers during his last season in Greece weren't great. He averaged just

9.5 points and 5.0 rebounds. But the Bucks liked his size and his skill. They took a chance and picked him fifteenth overall in the 2013 draft.

The decision changed the fortunes of the franchise and the face of the NBA. Antetokounmpo was 6 feet, 10 inches tall and weighed only 205 pounds when he was drafted. He filled out to 242 pounds after arriving in the NBA. And his wingspan measures 7 feet, 3 inches, which he uses to swallow up players defensively.

After a few years growing into his larger frame, Antetokounmpo became a star. He won his first MVP Award in 2018–19. Even better, he helped the Bucks improve to 60–22 under new coach Mike Budenholzer. In 2019–20 he won MVP and Defensive Player of the Year. Only NBA legends Michael Jordan and Hakeem Olajuwon had ever done that before.

Antetokounmpo didn't make it a three-peat as MVP in 2021. He claimed something even better. After the Bucks won their first title in 50 years, the superstar forward was MVP of the NBA Finals.

Even a player as special as Antetokounmpo couldn't win a title on his own. The Bucks put key pieces around him through the years. Khris Middleton was another unlikely star. The small forward was a second-round pick in 2012 by the Detroit Pistons. In his first season, he played only 27 games. But like Redd, Middleton grew from a second rounder into a star.

Khris Middleton made his first All-Star team in 2018–19.

The Bucks traded for him before the 2013–14 season. By the time he helped the Bucks win the title, he had been named to two All-Star teams. The accurate shooter averaged more than 20 points per game for the third time during Milwaukee's special run in 2020–21.

CHAPTER FOUR

MILWAUKEE MOMENTS

The Bucks lost only two games in three playoff rounds on their way to the 1971 title. Along the way, Kareem Abdul-Jabbar was establishing himself as the best center in the NBA.

Abdul-Jabbar had to face off with three future Hall-of-Fame centers in the playoffs. In the first round, he brushed aside a strong defender, Nate Thurmond of the San Francisco Warriors.

The second round brought a matchup with one of the greatest players of all time. Wilt Chamberlain had been the NBA's dominant center since joining the league in 1959. He had even befriended a young Abdul-Jabbar when the future Buck was a teenager in New York City. But when they met on the court, it was a changing of the guard for the NBA. The two players took shots at each other's play in the media and then on the scoresheet. Abdul-Jabbar came out on top, averaging

Kareem Abdul-Jabbar shows off his signature "skyhook" shot.

Fabulous 50

The Bucks' easy run to a title in 1971 produced some lopsided games. In Game 5 of the Western Conference semifinals against the San Francisco Warriors, the Bucks closed out the series with a 136–86 victory. Milwaukee led by 20 after the first quarter and kept right on going. The win was the franchise's biggest-ever blowout in the playoffs.

25.0 points and 17.2 rebounds in the Bucks' five-game victory.

In the Finals, Abdul-Jabbar matched up with Wes Unseld of the Baltimore Bullets. Unseld had a strong series, but Abdul-Jabbar was dominant. He showed the Bullets what they were up against right away. The Bucks center shot 13-for-16 in Game 1. His 31 points and 17 rebounds paced Milwaukee to a 98–88 victory. Nine days later, he threatened a triple-double, finishing with 27 points, 12 rebounds, and seven assists as the Bucks finished off the sweep 118–106.

BEATING THE BOGEYMAN

By 1986 Don Nelson's Bucks had a problem. Getting to the playoffs was a breeze. But beating the Philadelphia 76ers was a lot tougher. The 76ers knocked Milwaukee out of the postseason in 1981, 1982, 1983, and 1985. When Milwaukee fell behind 2–1 in the 1986 Eastern Conference semifinals, it looked as if it might happen again. Even worse, star guard Sidney Moncrief left the series with an injured heel.

Terry Cummings shot 12-for-19 in Game 7 of the 1986 Eastern Conference semifinals against the Philadelphia 76ers.

The rest of the Bucks rallied to win the next two games. But Philadelphia forced a Game 7 in Milwaukee. There the Bucks got a huge boost. Moncrief shook off the pain and started. He scored 23 points, while Terry Cummings added 27.

The game came down to the final seconds. With the Bucks leading 113–112, Philadelphia guard Sedale Threatt took the pass and dribbled to his left, drawing a double-team. He spotted forward Julius Erving open at the elbow for a jumper.

The future Hall-of-Famer's shot bounced off the rim and fell to the floor with two seconds left. Philadelphia forward Charles Barkley and Milwaukee point guard Ricky Pierce both fell on top of it. Time expired as they wrestled for the ball.

The Bucks had finally done it. And Milwaukee proved the win was no fluke the next year. The Bucks beat the 76ers in a five-game opening-round series in 1987.

BIG GAME FOR THE BIG THREE

Milwaukee was looking for any kind of playoff memory entering the 2001 postseason. The Bucks had not won a playoff round since 1988–89. But behind Glenn Robinson, Sam Cassell, and Ray Allen, Milwaukee put together a strong run.

The Bucks beat the Orlando Magic in four games in the opening round. Then they survived a tight seven-game series with the Charlotte Hornets. That put Milwaukee through to the Eastern Conference finals. Once again, the Philadelphia 76ers were waiting.

Led by superstar guard Allen Iverson, the 76ers took a 3–2 lead into the Bradley Center in Milwaukee for Game 6. Ray Allen started slowly in the game. He missed the only shot he took in the game's first six minutes. But his teammates picked him up. When Allen finally got on the board with 5:16 left, his shot made it 16–11. The made bucket woke the superstar guard up. He scored the next 17 Milwaukee points as well. After Allen's run was over, the Bucks led 33–15 early in the second quarter.

Allen was nowhere near finished. Milwaukee scored 35 points in the second. The sharpshooting guard finished it off by hitting back-to-back three-pointers. Milwaukee led 60–31 at the half.

Iverson responded in the fourth quarter with an amazing 26 points of his own. But it was too little, too late. The Bucks cruised to a 110–100 victory behind Allen's 41 points. One of the best three-point shooters in NBA history, Allen finished 9-for-13 from beyond the arc to tie a league playoff record.

Ray Allen (34) takes a jump shot over Philadelphia's Allen Iverson during the 2001 Eastern Conference finals.

THE BLOCK

One of the reasons the alley-oop is such an effective play is that if it is done correctly, the shot is nearly impossible to block. But in Game 4 of the 2021 NBA Finals, Giannis Antetokounmpo proved it can be done—and he did it at the most important time.

Wildcat Strike

One of Milwaukee's most impactful moments came in a game they chose not to play. In August 2020, the Bucks were participating in the NBA playoff bubble in Orlando, Florida. On August 23, a Black man named Jacob Blake was shot and paralyzed by police in Kenosha, Wisconsin, just south of Milwaukee. In protest of the shooting, the Bucks decided to go on strike and not play Game 5 of their series with the Orlando Magic. Their actions spurred other NBA teams to do the same in what is known as a "Wildcat Strike." For three days, there were no games while players protested police violence in the United States.

The Phoenix Suns entered Game 4 in Milwaukee up 2–1 in the series. None of the first three games had been close. But the Bucks held a slim 101–99 lead with 1:23 left in Game 4. Milwaukee had rallied from a nine-point deficit early in the fourth quarter.

Phoenix had the ball, and point guard Chris Paul passed to Suns center Deandre Ayton at the top of the key. Shooting guard Devin Booker then curled around Ayton and took a handoff pass. Booker slipped away from his defender as Ayton cut to the basket. Antetokounmpo moved off Ayton to cut off Booker's path to the basket. Booker flipped a lob over Antetokounmpo's head. As the ball sailed toward Ayton's outstretched hands, the Bucks defender wheeled around. Antetokounmpo slid back under the basket, rose up, and swatted the ball away as Ayton tried to slam it home.

The crowd, which included Bucks legends Oscar Robertson, Kareem Abdul-Jabbar, Jon McGlocklin, and Bob Dandridge,

Giannis Antetokounmpo (34) rejects Phoenix Suns center Deandre Ayton late in Game 4 of the 2021 NBA Finals.

went wild. Milwaukee held on for a 109–103 victory on the back of Antetokounmpo's incredible play.

The Bucks never lost again in the series. Within six days, Milwaukee was a city of champions for the first time in a half-century.

TIMELINE

1968
Milwaukee is awarded an NBA franchise on January 22. Four months later, the team is officially named the Bucks.

1969
The Bucks draft center Kareem Abdul-Jabbar from UCLA with the first pick in the draft.

1971
The Bucks lose only two playoff games on their way to winning the franchise's first NBA title.

1974
The Bucks reach the NBA Finals for the second time but fall in seven games to the Boston Celtics. Point guard Oscar Robertson retires after the series.

1975
The Bucks finish below .500 without Robertson. Abdul-Jabbar is traded to the Los Angeles Lakers after the season.

1976
Don Nelson makes his NBA head coaching debut. He coaches the Bucks through the 1986–87 season.

1979
The Bucks draft future All-Star guard Sidney Moncrief fifth overall.

1986
Terry Cummings scores 27 points as the Bucks edge Philadelphia 113–112 in Game 7 of the Eastern Conference semifinals.

1992

The Bucks finish 31–51 and miss the playoffs for the first time since the 1978–79 season.

1994

The Bucks draft forward Glenn "Big Dog" Robinson with the number one overall pick.

2001

Despite guard Ray Allen's playoff-record nine three-pointers in Game 6 of the Eastern Conference finals, the Bucks lose the series 4–3 to the Philadelphia 76ers.

2013

The Bucks select 18-year-old Giannis Antetokounmpo with the fifteenth pick in the NBA Draft.

2019

The Bucks finish 60–22 behind league MVP Antetokounmpo and win their first playoff series in 18 years by sweeping the Detroit Pistons in the first round.

2020

Antetokounmpo is named NBA MVP for the second season in a row.

2021

The Bucks erase a 2–0 series deficit in the NBA Finals against the Phoenix Suns, winning four straight games to capture the team's first NBA title since 1971.

TEAM FACTS

FRANCHISE HISTORY
Milwaukee Bucks (1968–)

NBA CHAMPIONSHIPS
1971, 2021

KEY PLAYERS
Kareem Abdul-Jabbar (1969–75)
Ray Allen (1996–2003)
Giannis Antetokounmpo (2013–)
Terry Cummings (1984–89, 1995–96)
Bob Dandridge (1969–77, 1981–82)
Marques Johnson (1977–84)
Khris Middleton (2013–)
Sidney Moncrief (1979–89)
Michael Redd (2000–11)
Oscar Robertson (1970–74)
Glenn Robinson (1994–2002)
Jack Sikma (1986–91)

KEY COACHES
Mike Budenholzer (2018–)
Larry Costello (1968–76)
Don Nelson (1976–87)

HOME ARENAS
MECCA Arena (1968–88)
    Known as:
    Milwaukee Arena (1968–74)
Bradley Center (1988–2018)
Fiserv Forum (2018–)

TEAM TRIVIA

BIG SHOES TO FILL

Hall of Fame center Bob Lanier spent the final five seasons of his career with the Bucks before retiring in 1984. Lanier wore size 22 shoes, the largest of any player in NBA history.

BINGO BANGO

Milwaukee's mascot is a deer named Bango. He was first introduced in 1977. The name comes from Eddie Doucette, the team's original radio announcer. Doucette was known for yelling "Bango!" after a Bucks player hit a long jump shot.

SHOOTING STAR

Giannis Antetokounmpo became the first Milwaukee player to win the NBA All-Star Game MVP Award. He claimed the honor in 2021 after scoring 35 points while making all 16 of his shots.

THE END OF THE ROAD

Julius Erving might have been an NBA star for the Philadelphia 76ers, but he was originally drafted by the Bucks. Milwaukee took Erving twelfth overall in 1972. However, the forward refused to sign, as he was already playing with the Virginia Squires of the rival American Basketball Association. Erving later joined the 76ers in the NBA. Instead of starting his career in Milwaukee, Erving's career ended there. Philadelphia's Game 5 loss in the opening round of the 1987 playoffs at Milwaukee's Bradley Center was the final game of his career.

GLOSSARY

alley-oop
A lob pass thrown from one player to another player jumping at the rim, who then either lays the ball in or dunks it.

assist
A pass that leads directly to a basket.

berth
A spot in a competition or tournament earned through previous results.

contender
A person or team that has a good chance of winning a championship.

draft
A system that allows teams to acquire new players coming into a league.

elbow
The corner where the free-throw line meets the side of the lane.

expansion
The addition of new teams to increase the size of a league.

layup
An easy shot made from close to the basket.

lockout
A work stoppage during which owners bar the players from playing or practicing.

overtime
An extra period of play when the score is tied after regulation.

rebound
To catch the ball after a shot has been missed.

triple-double
Accumulating 10 or more of three certain statistics in a game.

MORE INFORMATION

BOOKS

Flynn, Brendan. *The NBA Encyclopedia for Kids*. Minneapolis, MN: Abdo Publishing, 2022.

Mahoney, Brian. *GOATs of Basketball*. Minneapolis, MN: Abdo Publishing, 2022.

Ybarra, Andres. *Great Basketball Debates*. Minneapolis, MN: Abdo Publishing, 2019.

ONLINE RESOURCES

To learn more about the Milwaukee Bucks, please visit **abdobooklinks.com** or scan this QR code. These links are routinely monitored and updated to provide the most current information available.

INDEX

Abdul-Jabbar, Kareem, 16–18, 25–27, 35–36, 40
Allen, Ray, 20–22, 28–29, 38–39
Antetokounmpo, Giannis, 6, 7–8, 11–13, 22–23, 31–32, 39–41
Ayton, Deandre, 40

Barkley, Charles, 38
Blake, Jacob, 40
Booker, Devin, 5–6, 8–11, 40
Bridgeman, Junior, 28
Budenholzer, Mike, 11, 32

Cassell, Sam, 21–22, 29–31, 38
Catchings, Harvey, 28
Chamberlain, Wilt, 35
Costello, Larry, 18
Cummings, Terry, 28, 37

Dandridge, Bob, 17, 40

Embry, Wayne, 16
Erving, Julius, 37

Harris, Del, 20
Hodges, Craig, 28
Holiday, Jrue, 8–12

Iverson, Allen, 38–39

Johnson, Marques, 28
Jordan, Michael, 32

Karl, George, 20, 22
Kohl, Herb, 22

McGlocklin, Jon, 17, 40
Middleton, Khris, 6, 32
Moncrief, Sidney, 18–20, 27, 36–37

Nelson, Don, 18, 27, 36

Olajuwon, Hakeem, 32

Paul, Chris, 6, 8, 11–12, 40
Pierce, Rick, 28, 38
Popovich, Gregg, 11

Redd, Michael, 31–32
Robertson, Oscar, 17–18, 26–27, 40
Robinson, Glenn, 20–22, 28–29, 38

Threatt, Sedale, 37
Thurmond, Nate, 35

Unseld, Wes, 36

ABOUT THE AUTHOR

Will Graves has worked for more than two decades as a sports journalist and since 2011 has served as correspondent for The Associated Press in Pittsburgh, Pennsylvania, where he covers the National Hockey League, the National Football League, and Major League Baseball, as well as various Olympic sports.